AF430912

World in 2040

Prologue

This is an account on future predictions based on my research and my personal assumptions. As a disclaimer, I would like to note that these predictions should not be taken literally. However, there are merely projections that seem likely and by a large part are based on research.

In my references section you can see that I´ve relied heavily on the content of futuretimeline.net, which is website that publishes future predictions.

It is also worth mentioning that also my personal opinions regarding the future are based by logical conclusions, the history and the present factors.

Legal Disclaimer

None of the source material has been quoted directly but only referred to. These sources have been extensively documented in the references section found at the end of the book.

Wherein applicable, this book is subject to automatic copyright protection as an original work.

Table of Contents

Economy 8

   The Battle for the Leading Currency................................9

   India's Economy Reaches the Levels of USA and China 10

   Automation...11

   Jobs that have emerged 13

   Retail Industry transformation 14

   Mining Industry Revamp 15

   World's First Trillionaire has Emerged 16

   50% of shopping malls in United States have closed 17

   Most of British residents are now renting accommodation 18

Technology 19

   Artificial intelligence......................................20

   Robots..21

   Telepathic communication 22

   Carbon nanotube use is now commercially viable.........23

   16k virtual reality has become wildly popular 24

   6G is released 25

Space Achievements.......................................26

Permanent lunar base is established 27

Life outside earth detected 28

China Rivals the US in space race 29

Stark increase in space industry market value 30

Submarine exploration of Titan.....................................31

ISS is deorbited 32

Exponential growth of orbiting satellites 33

Energy 34

Green Energy...35

Hydrogen Network 36

NASA Launches Uranus Mission 37

Orbital solar energy is now commercially efficient.......38

India's reusable launch vehicle begins operations.......39

Entertainment 40

Immersive Video Games...41

Television and holographic entertainment technology ...42

Politics..43

Artificial Intelligence in Politics.....................................44

Fall of the European Union...45

Russia becomes a food superpower...............................46

Environment 47

Animal Endangerments and Extinctions.........................48

Deforestation..49

Climate Change 50

Another tipping point for permafrost melting reached 51

Extreme heat waves become the norm in the United States 52

All the ocean floor has been mapped 53

The idea of "Gene drive mosquitoes" becomes a reality 54

A volcanic eruption in Japan causes a large disaster 55

Gulf Coast cities are abandoned due to super hurricanes 56

Bangkok is largely underwater 57

Peak phosphorous reached 58

Earthquake devastates California 59

Social Sphere 60

Social Credit Score 61

Universal Basic Income 62

Increasing Poverty 63

Demographics 64

Demographic shift 65

The shaping of global population 66

Married Couples are now a Minority in the United Kingdom 67

Global child mortality has reached 2% 68

Health 69

Banning of tobacco 70

Breakthrough in battling diseases 71

Stem cell therapy 72

Robotic surgeries 73

Bionic Implants 75

Synthetic human genome is achieved 76

Food and Water 77

Plant based meat is dominating the meat market 78

Drinking water scarcity 79

Transportation 80

Self-driving cars 81

Airplane innovations 82

Flying Cars are Widespread in Urban Surroundings 83

Hyperloop 84

Northeast Corridor high-speed rail route completed 85

Helsinki-Tallinn tunnel has been completed 86

Cargo Sous Terrain construction is nearing its completion 87

Driverless flying taxis can be spotted everywhere 88

ICE transition into battery-electric shipping 89

All J.R.R. Tolkien's works are about to enter public domain 91

Possible Prediction Issues 92

Inaccurate predictions 93

Reasons why there MIGHT NOT BE A YEAR 2040 for us 94

References: 95

Economy

The Battle for the Leading Currency

The world economy has shaped itself significantly by the year 2040. Chinese and Indian economies have boomed and have not only caught up to the economy of the United States, but clearly left it behind. The gross domestic products of China and India now make a large portion of the global GDP.

The Chinese renminbi had earlier become the world's strongest currency and was now fighting with the Indian rupee for the title of the world's strongest currency.

Many might remember that for many decades, the US dollar was dominating as the lead currency. The global economic changes have altered that dynamic, predominantly due to the rising middle class in countries such as India and China.

Of course, the oil rich countries will maintain the titles of having some of the strongest currencies. It's always useful to have capital being backed by a commodity that has a strong demand.

What this means to the previously dominating currencies like dollar, aren't currently circulating as widely as it used to. Also, as a certain currency is losing its presence, it often starts devaluating.

There are also digital currencies adding their spin in the mix. One of the most obvious examples of digital currency is cryptocurrency. Probably the most famous bit of cryptocurrency is Bitcoin, which has been steadily gaining value throughout the decades. Other digital currencies are virtual currency and central bank digital currency. The more these digital currencies are in use, the more the less valuable traditional currencies become and that is just natural.

India's Economy Reaches the Levels of USA and China

During the last decades India has prospered greatly through efficient international trade negotiations coming from the public sector and strong business growth in the private sector.

Most of the world's wealth is distributed between China, India and the United States. India's edge has been lacking any population restrictions, effective fiscal policy, relatively low average age of its population and strong technical orientation of the major industries.

India has also strengthened its position on the world stage by gaining a permanent seat on the UN Security Council. It has become a prominent geopolitical player challenging U.S. and China on every level.

Economically speaking, India has a distinct advantage due to its market-based economy, versus the planned economy of China. As such, the value of rupee has increased tremendously and is in par with US dollar and China's renminbi.

India is also gaining ground in digital currency arena. India's central bank digital currency more commonly known as digital rupee. A couple decades ago, India launched a pilot project aimed at testing its new digital currency. It quickly became a viable alternative to its more traditional counterpart; the Indian rupee that was represented in banknotes and coins.

Digital rupee is also the official cryptocurrency of the Reserve Bank of India. Cryptocurrency is based on blockchain technology and is in the same category as Bitcoin. The cryptocurrencies, more commonly known as cryptos, have gained much more presence and influence in the global financial markets over the recent decades.

Automation

The industrial automation has become a norm in factories around the world, as robotic workforce has widely replaced the human workers and the new regulations have forbidden the human workforce to participate in several processes due to their potential hazards.

The automation takes shape in more and more sophisticated equipment that populates the factory floors and other premises. The automated machines work on voice command.

Jobs that have disappeared

There are much less jobs available in several industrial sectors compared to the early 21st century. The automated equipment has brought tremendous savings for companies, enabling them to produce products faster, cheaper and with higher quality.

Jobs that don't exist anymore

- **Mail Distributers**
  Postal packages are shipped via drones and the common figure such as "postman" has disappeared into the archives of history books. Deliveries are now made by mail delivery robots and drones. Every now and then there are cases where some hooligans decide to harm these vehicles. However, due to the biometric recognition scanners on each of these vehicles, the identities of these individuals are spotted and reported immediately.

- **Taxi Drivers**

  You might remember when you were scanning the street for a yellow cab to wave to? Now it's all changed. These days all the cars are driverless, and you can easily call a driverless taxi and it will be with you in just a few minutes. Your automated vehicle already knows where you're heading before you step in and you'll be able to enjoy a relaxing ride. Also, the number of personal drivers have been reduced due to safety issues and convenience.

- **Truck Drivers**

  Truck driving has once been one of the most common jobs in countries such as the United States. The average truck driver earns approximately $50,000 a year and truck operating companies have seen that as a redundant expense. Truck drivers tend to drive long hours and every now and then especially sleep deprived drivers cause an accident or happen to arrive late. Self driving trucks have removed that risk and are now able to drive non-stop without delays, only stopping at electric charging stations every now and then.

- **Farmers**

  Farmers have indeed disappeared as automated farming machines are conducting the crop production. Also, cattle is being handled by the robots and human workforce has been excluded. The automated farming also ensures higher product quality and faster work delivery.

- **Call Centre Operators**

  The tasks that used to be the bread and butter of a human operator, such as customer and technical support are now easily being handled by the software powered by artificial intelligence.

Jobs that have emerged

There are a number of jobs that have emerged to compliment the disappearance of some of the jobs. These jobs often provide high value and user input to the highly developed technical environments accompanied by artificial intelligence.

- **VR Architect**
  The responsibility of a VR Architect is to utilize the virtual reality to model new artificial maps, components and designs used for industrial and consumer driven purpose.
- **Nanotech Manufacturer**
  The nanotechnology has evolved to the state of becoming active and interactive in terms of its functionalities to the point that they are able to sense and process and, in some cases, even auto-repair.
- **Biohacking Guru**
  A biohacking guru, or a programmable healthcare guru is someone that is able to utilize biological programming in order to achieve better health and even cure a significant portion of disease on a genetic level.
- **Robot Specialist**
  There are multiple complex robots, and it requires a specialist to handle one of the multiple areas relating to robots. Some specialists take on development, others do maintenance, third take care of the psychological aspect.

Retail Industry transformation

When it comes to retail industry, the leading player is Amazon. There have been attempts to challenge Amazon's market leading position, but to no avail. Brick and mortar-type of outlets have become increasingly rare, especially in less densely populated areas.

However, the metropolitan areas have still retained their status as business hubs, tending to the needs of clients that still look forward to the traditional shopping experience. However, instead of using cash and credit cards, people simply walk by special sensors that remove the balance of their acquired items from their bank accounts instantaneously.

The way this works, is that each consumer has a special smart device attached to him that interacts with the sensors acting as your smart wallet.

Amazon Go was one of the first ones to delve into the future retail shopping through in a brick-and-mortar store. The way it worked was having an app installed with your phone, connected with your wallet and by scanning your QR code you could enter and exit the shop without having to touch your actual physical wallet or the cash and credit or debit cards in it.

Sweden on the other hand was one of the first countries to try it with implantable microchips, to make way for even lower effort cashless transactions. This paved the way for future innovations where the promise was to make the life easier with a compounding focus easier.

Mining Industry Revamp

The mining industry has had significant leaps in innovations within the last few decades. All the mining activities are now automated and performed by robots. Even such far reaching ventures as space mining have now become commercially viable. The wealthiest mining companies have already established their presence in space and making billions of dollars.

At the same time, deep ocean mining has become commercially viable and also highly popular among mining companies. Deep sea mining got its origins from 60's of the past century and the prospects for it started improving along with lowering of the costs. At the turn of the millennium, there was only one particular item mined from the ocean and that item was diamonds. But as the time progressed, by 2040 the robotic innovations facilitated mining of vast amount of various different minerals from the ocean floor.

Some might argue that this focus on space and ocean mining is due to disappearance of those minerals from different pockets on the surface of the earth. While lots of those pockets have been effectively mined to the point that they don't produce more high valued precious metals and minerals, such assumption would be absurd. While many of the known locations have been successfully used up, there are still lots of places that even to this day are unknown that are rich and such deposits.

The population increase and also the increase of mean average income has had its effect on demand of jewellery and as we all know, supply tends to follow the demand.

World's First Trillionaire has Emerged

During the span of ever-increasing income inequality, world's first ever trillionaire has claimed the stake to a staggering wealth. This individual is a world-famous American business magnate. He has reached the status of a trillionaire by the end of 2030's.

The considerable amount of this wealth has been achieved through commercial space exploration and particularly through excavating rare metals and minerals from lunar surface and from the objects flying in the orbit of the earth.

The amount of trillionaires is estimated to be 10 by the year 2070.

The exponential wealth growth of the few select individuals has divided people in their opinions of such wealth accumulators. Some find them inspiring and are openly fans of them while the others find them repulsively and criticize them at every turn.

The trillionaires wield significant amount of influence, which shows in politics, social media and other areas. When we look at the earliest decades of 21st century, we've seen the types of Jeff Bezos, Richard Branson and Elon Musk venture into space, innovate electric cars and much more. But above all that, they have been popular media figures whose opinion is often significant.

The richest also often contribute to charitable causes sending massive donations to various developing nations and also spearheading projects that make a difference, improving the lives of numerous people.

Also, there has been a number of high net worth individuals who have consciously decided to give up majority of their wealth and that we can all appreciate.

50% of shopping malls in United States have closed

Shopping malls have been an integral part of the American culture throughout the better part of 1900's. Halfway through the 90's of last century 140 shopping malls were being built each year. That was the pinnacle of the shopping mall spree, a popular place for young people to hang out, kids to play and adults do their shopping.

But things were bound to change. And so, by the turn of the millennium, shopping malls slowly started emptying up. For the first time in 50 years 2007, one year before the financial meltdown, saw no new shopping malls being constructed anywhere in the United States. In the span of the next 5 years only one shopping mall was constructed in the States.

The causality to this sudden change roots deep in consumer habits. As the consumer became much more careful to spend their dollars and found the worldwide web's own shopping portals in sites such as Amazon.com and similar online stores where with just a few clicks of a mouse, a product could be delivered right to their doorstep.

Shopping malls haven't however emptied up completely. They still collect consumers who are eager to buy groceries or latest tech. They still gather to watch movies in a film theatre. They want to bring their kids to play in children's facilities and arcade rooms.

Despite the reduction in the construction of shopping malls, the malls are still here to stay, since they represent so much to the public that wants to experience different things inside them.

Most of British residents are now renting accommodation

By the early 2030's the prices of the United Kingdom houses were so high, that it was no longer affordable for most UK residents to purchase a home of their own and so they resorted to rent it instead.

The ability to pay monthly rent has now replaced the ability to pay mortgage. On the other hand, the tenants don't bear as great of a responsibility of the property condition as the owner.

On the other hand, the idea of ownership has greatly changed in the recent decades. If baby boomers were the epitome of spending on private property and materialistic tendencies, then the following generations became gradually more minimalistic by comparison.

The reason for such transformation is quite simple when you look at the change of lifestyle especially of the western population. As more and more aspects have become virtual, people are more fixated on the value of their virtual possessions rather than material ones.

Although the housing market is a market indeed and thus the prices fluctuate moving up and down depending on a wide range of factors, the overall trend especially closer to the densely inhabited areas has been generally upward.

Banks have also been pickier with mortgage requesters remembering the 2008 banking crisis where subprime mortgages were given out too easily and which in turn lead to collapse of the market and huge economic crash.

Also, it's quite obvious that those living on welfare or other type of benefits cannot afford to buy their own house and the amount of those has increased drastically.

Technology

Artificial intelligence

The A.I. has galvanized itself as the permanent part of information technology. As previously mentioned in the Automation segment, the A.I. has caused a vast displacement of a human workforce that has been forced to find new ways of earning income. Automatization hasn't only applied to the production industries but also to service industries.

The artificial intelligence technology is now able to handle customer service, cold calling as well as the help desk functions. Artificial intelligence has in integral role going into the future and it facilitates quite a lot of repetitive tasks, but on the other hand it's a big responsibility.

The responsibility, in this case, means the sheer task of maintaining the A.I. balance on one hand, so that it functions flawlessly and on the other hand, so that it won't cause harm to humanity.

The artificial intelligence is present in people's everyday lives in software that can be experienced in computers, smart homes, smart refrigerators in them, smart security systems and of course robots.

Robots are more widely described in the next chapter, but the way they operate is that they are moving mechanical entities that utilize artificial intelligence. With humanlike robots in place, the level of artificial intelligence is humongous.

The humanlike A.I. is designed to think, express ideas, thoughts and emotions which are simulated of course and often a response to your micro expressions, gestures, words, and such. This is something we could only dream about decades ago.

Robots

There are now more than 1 billion service robots in the world. Since we are currently exploring the year 2040. The threshold of 1 billion was reached in 2034, 6 years ago.

There are several different robot types. The robotics technology has significantly evolved from vacuum cleaner robots that were popular at the turn of the century. Nowadays robots are far more sophisticated and capable of carrying out complex intellectual and physical tasks.

A robot is designed not to do any harm to human beings. It uses principles or better yet, laws to implement its protective framework.

Some of us may have heard about Isaac Asimov's three laws of robotics. Those laws are (quoting the Wikipedia):

1. A robot may not injure a human being or, through inaction, allow a human being to come to harm.
2. A robot must obey the orders given it by human beings except where such orders would conflict with the First Law.
3. A robot must protect its own existence as long as such protection does not conflict with the First or Second Laws.

Those laws are in place to have so called safety guardrails that are aimed to prevent any harm coming from a robot. Of course, a robot can be hacked or reprogrammed or malfunction sometimes, but in most cases robots are safe.

Telepathic communication

Human thoughts seemed to be a very private matter. After all, sometimes they hid something in them that wasn't appropriate to be shared, for example. But who from the old days would have thought that speaking would someday become obsolete?

Thoughts are now like instant messages in the old days. You can convey information or process orders for example.

The technology is based on brain-computer interface, where one's brains are directly connected to communication technology and messages can be interchanged through wireless network. These brain-computer interfaces are first generations, which means it's a recent innovation and better versions are already being developed.

The biggest breakthrough in this technology were achieved by 2030, by unveiling the secrets of brains and the related neuroelectric signals.

Basically, similar type of communication has been invented long ago. Radio signals travel through radio waves while in order for humans to speak with technology, similar waves are created but it requires you to wear special headsets, visors and earphones, which quite small and very comfortable.

This is great news for those who are happen to be mute and cannot voice their thoughts in form of an audible speech.

Technically, the way it works, this technology catches your neuroelectric signals and transforms them into a message or a command. And with that, high detail real-time messages are within the realm of possibility in a way which is non-invasive.

Carbon nanotube use is now commercially viable

It took several decades of tireless research to come up with new processes for synthetic carbon nanotube that could bring a whole range of new innovations in engineering, architectural designs and scientific materials.

The carbon nanotube structures can reach the length of thousands of kilometres. Thanks to extensive purification methods, the highest level of tensile strength of carbon nanotube can be achieved, making it several hundred times stronger than steel for example.

Carbon nanotube can be used as a building material for many different things, among others – a space elevator. A space elevator is part of technology that innovates other methods of entering space without using propulsion vehicles, such as space shuttles.

Carbon nanotube has been applied in relatively small quantities from the early decades of 21st century. For example, Easton-Bell Sports Incorporated together with Zyvex Performance Materials has been using carbon nanotube tech to develop and produce a few of their bicycle parts, such as handlebars, forks and such.

Another good example is a company called Amroy Europe Oy, which manufactures Hybtonite carbon nanoepoxy resins, where the carbon nanotubes activate chemically, bonding to epoxy in the process and creating a composite material that is 20-30% stronger compared to any other composite material.

So, as you can see, there are plenty of uses for carbon nanotube, which is part of ever-increasing trend of developing nanotechnology, which has been greatly researched throughout the 21st century.

16k virtual reality has become wildly popular

In the early 2040, the virtual technology has been improved greatly since its early days. Almost fully immersive virtual reality can now be experienced in games and other VR applications.

As of now, most of the VR headsets now include 16K by default, which is a double compared to the pixel standard of 2030. At the same time, the average graphics processing unit in the early 2040's is exceeding 10 petaFLOPS (processing power), which to put it bluntly, is 1000 more efficient than in early 2020's.

Nowadays mainstream brain-computer interface has got the latest technological boost as well. When that is combined with human-like AI and 16K virtual reality resolution, the virtual experience becomes amazing.

Increasing the screen pixelation rate is a continuous trend, a working progress in other words. When we talk about 16k resolution, the more specific description is horizontal resolution and most commonly the display would be presented in 15360 × 8640. This totals to 132.7 megapixels. The earliest video card types that implemented 16k resolution for multi monitor setup were AMD Eyefinity and Nvidia Surround.

The very first company to present the 100-inch 16K8K display module was called Innolux. The next company to present its own version of 16k resolution was Sony.

The new screen resolution was adapter and welcomed with huge enthusiasm especially among the gaming community.

6G is released

By the year 2030, the world surpassed the old 5G network and was ready to take the next step in the technological development. With greater bandwidth and much lower latency, the 6G network was taken into consumption.

Back in the day, when 5G revolutionized the world of data transfer, some issues emerged with it. Namely, a huge demand for wireless data transfer caused mounting pressure on the service providers and caused a need for even shorter latencies.

That was the main cause for developing 6G. It was based on frequencies that ranged anywhere between 100 Gigahertz to 1 Teraherz. This led to tenfold increase in data transfer speed, which now is calculated in terabits per second. When you add the artificial intelligence into the mix, the reach of this 6G network is even more comprehensive.

It took around 10 years of development and testing before 6G was brought to market and when it was, it led to its mass adoption.

The 7G has been also considered as a new, subsequent standard, but it was discovered that it was highly difficult to surpass the terabits per second data transfer rate. Therefore, the following updates have become iterative in their nature, rather than generational.

So the internet connection speed will be increasing within the realistic framework based on the technological possibilities and there will be constantly new innovations relating to the internet technology.

Space Achievements

Permanent lunar base is established

By the year 2040, for the first time ever, a permanent human inhabited base has been established on the moon. This is a tremendous accomplishment for the science and space development in particular and it falls on the era of accelerated space engineering where major milestones have been achieved.

The base includes terraformed greenhouses inside domes and solar panels that provide continuous electricity to the base.

The first step towards building a permanent lunar base was to create a space station in lunar orbit, which was achieved by late 2020's. As a result, multiple robotic platforms were deployed to the surface of the moon to prepare for the base construction. The first operational lunar base was built in mid-2030's. This was done in collaboration with the European and Canadian space agencies as well as commercial organizations.

The permanent lunar base will allow the scientists stationed on it to explore moon and its surface in particular more closely and also to conduct experiments on it.

At the same time, there are commercial organizations that are building hotels on the moon. The guests will experience real lunar walks in space suits, zero gravity and luxurious food, beverages and entertainment. Of course, this will be a very pricey experience and thus will be reserved for the wealthiest.

The successful permanent lunar base will also lead to permanent base on planet Mars and there already are plans how to terraform the planet Mars.

Life outside earth detected

New evidence has been discovered that there´s actual life on one of the millions of exoplanets that have been discovered by our space investigation technology. The suitable chemical environment, consisting of oxygen, hydrogen and methane have been pinpointed by the A.I. using algorithms and utilizing a new HDST telescope, which is significantly superior to formerly known Hubble or Kepler telescopes.

Recording biosignatures has paid off and the evidence of life outside our solar system has been found, which has led to a deep religious and cultural impact on a global level. More money has been invested in the exploration of space and its increasingly more interesting planets.

There have of course been rumours that UFO's exist ever since the first sightings. This has led to wild conspiracy theories, and many have written extensive books based around this topic and there have even been multiple films relating to it.

However, there haven't been concrete hard evidence that would once and for all prove the existence of extra-terrestrial beings until this discovery. The finding resulted in widescale media coverage and many political pundits, podcasters and such have discussed it and its implications for humanity at length.

However, this new discovery inspires many and leads to more and more scientific discoveries.

China Rivals the US in space race

China has become the number one rival to the United States when it becomes to space race. The Chinese now have an impressive set of manned space fleet and an established base on the moon.

Chinese space travel companies are now offering interplanetary voyages as a comparatively lower cost compared to what its American counterparts are offering.

The largely nuclear-powered space transport vehicles can offer their guests a trip to Moon or even Mars.

As Chinese venture capitalists and grant programs have poured more funding into different space programs, that has opened doors for more and more common space explorations for scientific and commercial purposes. That expanded funding has lead to brand new technological innovations of which the west could only dream about.

The large-scale projects include mining on asteroids, building orbital solar power stations, launching long distance space explorations and much more.

At the early stages of Chinese efforts in the space race, it focused on building fully functional space stations in planet earth's orbit. In addition, many space exploratory efforts were undertaken by the Chinese space experts. And of course, China achieved its own permanent lunar base.

Based on the current trajectory, China will probably overtake the United States in space race and be the number one space faring nation.

Stark increase in space industry market value

Believe it or not, in the year 2040 the space industry is worth over 1 trillion dollars. There has been a rapid expansion in demand of high-speed web services over the past few decades. This has prompted increased amount of satellite technology development and deployment.

Another factor to the increasing value of space industry is space tourism that has become more affordable, and more mainstream compared to the past recent decades. Space tourism mainly features relatively short flights outside of earth's atmosphere to see the vastness of space, the stars, and the earth from space.

And of course, let's not forget the enormously lucrative space mining industry that has excavated space objects using their specialized mining technology.

All-in-all this is still just the beginning of the potential of human impact in space. Many of us have seen the movies where space travellers are suspended in cryogenic sleep. Cryogenic hibernation is actually not all fiction, but it's been used in reality. The initial applications of it were wealthy customers willing to freeze their body for later revival if or when the technology permits it.

Nowadays cryogenic hibernation is more and more popular not only for passing the long space travel hours but also for its health benefit. The scientific discoveries will lead to further increase in the space industry market value over the coming years.

Submarine exploration of Titan

China has become the number one rival to the United States when it becomes to space race. The Chinese now have an impressive set of manned space fleet and an established base on the moon.

When it comes to space craft technology, the highest leaps have been attained in the propulsion technology. The modern space craft is much faster in comparison with its predecessors, adding efficiency to the space travel.

And now, that space travel has brought the exploration on one of Milky way's planet's moons, namely a moon called Titan. Titan has often been a subject of enthusiastic conversations, and not only due to its impressive name, but that's also out of Greek mythology.

And that name is well deserved, since Titan is the largest moon orbiting planet Saturn and also the second largest natural satellite in our solar system.

Titan is the only planetary body other than Earth that has liquid lakes and seas. However, the difference is that on Titan, the lakes and seas consist of liquid methane instead of water. Temperatures of that liquid is almost -300 degrees Fahrenheit.

Thea idea of submarine exploration was developed by NASA along with Johns Hopkins Applied Physics Lab and Penn State University Applied Research Lab.

The underwater vessel would carry various instruments to measure the liquid composition of chemicals, underwater currents, different movements of the liquid bodies and such.

ISS is deorbited

The International Space Station, which started its operations back in 2000, has now reached its finish line. It was designed to endure only 15 years of operations. However, it remained functioning throughout 2010's and 2020's.

After many orbit time extensions, auxiliary modules and upgrade work was attributed to it, its lifespan doubled compared to its preliminary one.

The deorbited International Space Station will be downed onto Point Nemo in the Pacific Ocean upon its decommission. Point Nemo happens to be the furthers place from any inhabited location on the planet.

Deorbiting is not an easy undertaking. It requires careful planning and implementation. Deorbiting an entire space station is far more complicated than deorbiting a simple satellite.

The first step is removing all the valuable scientific equipment from the space station. It also requires removing the crew from the space station. The final part is controlled deorbiting process that is controlled from NASA headquarters.

And once the old space station is down, it's only a matter of time till the new one becomes operational. So, it becomes a smooth transition all things considered. The new space station will have more upgrades compared to the previous one. It will have more advanced equipment and it will be much safer as well.

Exponential growth of orbiting satellites

By the end of 2020's the number of satellites reached almost 60,000. That was a number that multiplied the number of satellites in earth's orbit by a factor of 20.

As we all know, the first satellite in history, the Russian Sputnik was launched in 1957. Only 3 years passed as a hundred other satellites were launched and while the Soviet Union and the United States started their competition for space dominance. During the decades that followed, more and more countries joined the race, launching their satellites to track the weather, enhance communication on earth, enhance military surveillance and finally to facilitate navigation through the famous GPS.

While the early satellites were relatively large and heavy, after the turn of the millennium, the satellites became smaller and easier to deploy. This led to more affordable satellite deployment as well as increased range of satellite application options. While the mini satellites could weight anywhere from a hundred to five hundred kilograms, the smaller ones – the femto models could weigh less than one tenth of a kilogram.

The abundance of satellites orbiting the earth has led to an accumulating debris problem mainly consisting of older and decommissioned satellites. This is a substantial problem especially for those that are building new space stations or planning to launch new satellites, as the debris can cause considerable damage to them by colliding with them.

That's why there has been an effort to clean up the orbit of the space debris. Many ideas have been presented but only few viable solutions have been proposed.

Energy

Green Energy

Technological solutions to improve energy efficiency and developing towards greener, sustainable energy have led to scientific breakthroughs, producing innovations, some of which were only vague ambitions in the early 21st century.

This whole green movement started when people came to realize how much of a risk the non-renewable energy was.

One of those ambitions was fusion power. Now, in the 2040, the fusion power is becoming commercially available. However, majority of power is being generated through renewable energy sources, such as wind, solar and water. Fossil fuel power plants have been shut down and people can breathe fresh air.

Another viable energy source is hydrogen. There's a vast hydrogen energy grid that has been constructed in developed countries. This type of energy is clean, renewable and much safer than nuclear energy.

Solar energy has been introduced many decades ago. It was first used in small personal applications such as calculators and on building roofs. Then there were solar parks and finally there are orbital solar stations. The energy produced is significant.

Wind power has been another form of green energy, but it used to have a big downside. It wasn't very energy efficient. Nowadays there is technology in place to make wind energy efficient.

This same principle applies to many other renewal energy sources. At the same time the world has dropped the majority of coal power plants and other non-renewable sources of energy.

Hydrogen Network

By 2040, hydrogen has been established as one of the most common clean energy sources. Essentially the hydrogen transport has been established through hydrogen pipelines built throughout Europe.

The pipeline runs through almost a dozen countries having a span of over 20,000 kilometres. The initiative for this new form of energy was created by desire to decrease the carbon producing energy plants and create a cleaner energy source.

And hydrogen is clean indeed. We've come a long way from the polluting coal power plants, first shifting to nuclear power and now leaning on more and more expansive hydrogen energy grid.

The world decided largely to move away from nuclear energy, due to its potential hazards. History remembers the meltdowns of nuclear reactors and how hazardous the outcome was to the surrounding environment.

Hydrogen is an excellent source of energy since it is abundant and easily renewable. If you add to that almost total lack of emissions coming out of utilizing hydrogen as a source of energy. It's not a surprise that hydrogen was early on used even as a fuel for vehicles.

The early stages of hydrogen energy network development included mapping out the technological aspects and cost related to this very comprehensive venture.

The hydrogen energy option has gained wide popularity around the world and it's production, distribution is use is relatively easy and secure.

NASA Launches Uranus Mission

This mysterious distant planet with hints of blue and green and it's two rings is a fascinating yet distant planet in our solar system. For many millennia, this planet was all but a distant piece in our solar constellation.

It wasn't until 1986, when Voyager 2, the NASA's space exploration spacecraft flew relatively close to the planet, that we finally got a better look at this beautiful planet.

The launch itself was initially planned between years 2030 and 2034. However, due to delays and budgetary issues, the launch kept being postponed and the final factor in redesignating a new launch window was NASA's Space Launch System, a brand-new propulsion spacecraft rocket system that would decrease the Uranus travel time by 4 years. Thus, the trip to Uranus would take only 8 years in total.

As one of the coldest locations in our solar system, Uranus is a challenging exploration ground. It houses water, ammonia and methane at extremely cold temperatures.

The first close proximity investigation of the planet was made in 1986 when Voyager 2 passed by at a distance of less than 100,000 kilometers from Uranus.

The Uranus missions were in early planning stages ever since NASA and European Space Agency had preliminary discussions of it in early 2000's.

By the early 2040's Uranus mission is ongoing, providing valuable information about the atmosphere, inner composition, rings and other scientific data of Uranus. The moons of the planet are also documented in high detail.

Orbital solar energy is now commercially efficient

After years and years, the solar energy is now powering several electrical grids.

The solar power technology has been available since the 70's of the previous century. However, it was never commercial feasible up until now.

The solar energy is generated by solar panels on large satellites in earth's orbit. Those panels are nanotechnology based and span between 1 – 3 km in size. The solar panels absorb the sunlight and then transmit it to earth through microwave radiation or via lasers. The earth's satellite dishes receive it and transform into energy. The power can be directed to several different locations on earth depending on the requirements.

This technology has led to higher rate of energy collection, while also increasing the collection duration. Weather is no longer a factor, when it comes to energy collection. Also, this type of technology has doesn't harm the environment of the earth. It's a green solution providing fully renewable energy and decreasing the need for non-renewable and harmful energy sources.

The panels are highly durable against various objects bumping into them in space. The latest developments in nanotechnology that are implemented in the panels allow them to repair automatically whenever they have been damaged by space debris for example.

India's reusable launch vehicle begins operations

During the last couple of decades, Indian Space Research Organization has developed a two stage to orbit reusable launch vehicle.

The first prototype which was developed back in 2016 reached the speed of Mach 5 and an altitude of 65 kilometers.

In 2023 India had succeeded propelling its astronauts into space using a little capsule attached to a rocket with the reusable launch system. A successful launch has led to much lengthier, more advanced space missions by Indian astronauts while greatly reducing the cost.

This could be considered a spinoff from SpaceX developed reusable launch rockets that were developed with enormous amount of determination, and which took a while to accomplish. However, the Indian space ambitions required their own approach to more affordable space ventures.

Nevertheless, this is a substantial step towards more sustainable space travel. Many of us remember, how in the early days of space faring rockets and the decades that followed, the first stage separated from the second stage. One of them continued its bath, the other one, the first stage, drops towards earth and subsequently burns in its atmosphere.

This costly and potentially hazardous maneuver is now in the past as more and more space vehicles have switched to reusable launch systems.

Entertainment

Immersive Video Games

The video game technology has reached such levels of artificial reality that it's virtually indistinguishable from it. The graphics are razor sharp and the amount of pixilation is immense.

What used to be the VR-goggles is now full spectrum virtual reality experience, has turned into fully immersive virtual reality, where the player can move in an actual virtual world and shoot the bad guys or construct objects using virtual building materials and tools.

Nowadays video games aren't only a method of entertaining the young and the youthful, but it can be also a used as a powerful learning tool. Many of those who aspire to get a driver's licence can now practice their driving skills in very realistic virtual environment.

As they say it's all fun and games, but the downside is that people are spending more time playing games and more and more gamers are there to play together online and separately.

On the other hand, there are more and more opportunities to earn money by playing games and by combining playing games with social media.

Despite gigantic leaps in developing as realistic games as possible, the range of genres has pretty much remained the same. We still have the pulse jolting action games, the first person and third person shooters, fantastic fantasy games, horrifying horror games, useful simulation games, tactical strategy games, adrenaline inducing racing games, sports games and similar games.

The game functionalities, however, have broadened significantly. Now there are more multi-dimensional games where each individual choice made by player affects the continuation of the game.

Television and holographic entertainment technology

The flat screen TV's that were in almost every household in the early 2000's, have now become obsolete. The normal flatscreen technology was replaced by 3D screens, plasma screens, curved screens and even folding screens. Now smart walls can take the shape of the screen in smart apartments.

Also, holographic image projection has now become widespread. This is very convenient because the audience can observe a news broadcast, movies or series 360 degrees around the holographic projection.

The holographic image projection has been utilized for other purposes as well, apart from TV entertainment. Video games can also be played utilizing this holographic technology. Along with virtual reality tools, the gameplay has become very immersive.

Holographic technology can also be used very practically. A virtual assistant, similar to Amazon Alexa back in the first decade of 2000's, is now available as a holographic man or woman just like in the film Blade Runner 2049.

Holoprojectors can produce a large scale hologram for a large auditorium, where the audience in many cases surrounds the projection instead of sitting in multiple rows facing it.

But all-in-all, the hologram is not a replacement for flatscreen display, it's just an alternative. And the ultra-realistic 16k screens that are currently widespread attract a huge amount of consumers that are prepared to spend on the sharpest display realistic in the market. The abundance of choice among high definition display types is of course one of the perks of the futuristic new age.

Politics

Artificial Intelligence in Politics

Several sources have been warning of serious dangers that the Artificial Intelligence might bring. For example, in an article published by the CNBC, some research in the Rand Corporation claimed that the Artificial Intelligence might lead to a nuclear war by 2040. This prediction turned out to be incorrect, as the A.I. was never allowed to make major global scale decisions in the public sector.

The A.I., however, has been employed to analyse the statistics and decision making in a historical context and given advisory tasks to produce data for the governmental bodies in several countries across Europe, Americas, and Asia.

There are several other benefits to the artificial intelligence as well. Some of them are detecting any corruption and reporting it immediately. Also, the artificial intelligence helps to analyse political candidates by checking their background for example. The artificial intelligence can also increase the productivity of a public sector program by checking it for any loopholes or other issues.

From information standpoint, the AI can easily fact check every bit of news that is being reported and weed out the factually incorrect news stories.

From cost saving perspective, the artificial intelligence could save a lot of tax payer money, because the AI can be employed to do office tasks just as any office worker that is on the government payroll. By reducing the workforce, the government offices will not only become affordable but also more efficient.

Fall of the European Union

The Union that was formed after the Second World War, has faced severe challenges ever since the new millennium. 20 years after that, the Great Britain left the European Union based on a majority vote by the British people. The challenges have mostly been of political nature focusing on issues, such as mass immigration and economy. However, currently the climate change has become the new player on the horizon of the ever-growing political unrest.

What was left from the previously known European Union, had become known as "Northern Union" that included France, Germany, Scandinavia, Benelux countries along with Poland. Now even this coalition is on its last breath.

For years, the climate change refugees have been escaping especially the Northern African regions up north, to find a lifeline on the better pastures so to say. The long and hazardous migration trips have often had fatal consequences but have also permanently changed the European demographics.

Europe's economic policies, especially the united currency Euro has brought lots of issues especially during the time when some southern European Euro zone members struggled financially to the extent that the wealthier nations had to bail them out collectively.

Also, the European immigration policy in many cases has rubbed many people, especially nationalistic factions within them the wrong way. This has led to many populist candidates emerging in the political spectrum, some of whom even became elected into the public office of considerable power and responsibility.

Russia becomes a food superpower

As the world population nears 9 billion, the food production needs to be ramped up by 50% compared to early 2000's. As the need for food production is imminent the peak phosphorous and climate change effects are causing concern.

Russia has often been famed as one of the top producers of certain consumer products, which are exported worldwide. As the largest country in the world, it also has a large array of abundant resources and rich plains to grow crops and to farm cattle.

Russia has also maintained political self-sufficiency and independence from different governing bodies such as the European Union. Russia has maintained a strong position as in on itself and as a part of economic coalitions such as BRICS.

Russia has also maintained highly nationalistic policies in many aspects, particularly when it comes to their resources. For decades Russia has strived to be self-sufficient and independent from influence coming from overseas.

As the top food producer, Russia has also had the option to fix the prices, especially on certain food products. However, the prices have commonly been regulated mostly by market conditions, tariffs and other such factors that have affected the price in the previous decades.

Some other countries have been trying to offset largescale dependency on large scale food imports from Russia by incentivising local production. However, in many cases the changed environmental conditions on a large part caused by global warming have caused such efforts to be futile.

Environment

Animal Endangerments and Extinctions

Several well-known animal species have become extinct, including hundreds of butterfly species and over a half of the polar bears of the Antarctic compared to their numbers half a century ago. Poachers have caused a tremendous toll on the number of elephants.

Several different animal species in the oceans, lakes and rivers as well as different types of mammals will become highly endangered.

As of 2040, within a few decades the majority of primate species will be eradicated from the wilderness. This has been primarily brought by continuous construction and expansion of human territory taking out the habitat of various primate species. Poaching is also a significant factor.

By 2040, elephants are on the brink of extinction. These big friendly animals have brought joy to people for thousands of years as well as been instruments of warfare and public entertainment in zoos.

Hundreds of species have been either extinct or are close to extinction in 2040, compared to two decades ago. The scientists have been alarmed not only by this, but also by the trickling down domino effect that mass extinction has triggered.

The domino effect takes down pieces of food chain that have been established during the long periods of animal presence on the planet. And the more pieces get removed from the food chain, the more the domino effect gets accelerated.

That's why it's important to cherish the animals that we currently have and do everything we can to preserve the animal sustainability on our planet.

Deforestation

Close to 50% of the South America's rain forest, comparing to the beginning of 21st century, has disappeared due to industrial harvesting. There have been some efforts to mitigate the effects of deforestation through planting trees.

Over one third of the initial Congo Jungle has been harvested into oblivion. At the turn of millennium, the Congo Jungle amounted to nearly 25% of all the tropical forests in the world.

The forests are a significant part of creating oxygen through photosynthesis and providing a home to countless animal species as well as indigenous tribes.

According to National Geographic's encyclopaedic definition, "Deforestation is the intentional clearing of forested land".

The habit of cutting trees has been around for thousands of years, ever since humans invented fire and started building tools and buildings out of wood. In the early days, there was abundance of trees and cutting them did not affect things in a major scale.

Later, as the tree consumption scaled up, the trees became a major product and, in some cases, trees had to be imported from other regions. Nowadays trees are being cut to an extent where the damage especially to animal species in some cases becomes permanent.

Efficient ways of helping prevent deforestation is decreasing consumption of different paper products, such as toilet paper and printing paper. There are many ways to support the forests and many companies are already limiting their printing paper consumption.

Climate Change

By 2040, the average world temperature has gone up by nearly 2°C from the levels it had only a couple decades ago. There is a tremendous concern about the repercussions of the continuing climate change.

As it was denominated at the UN Climate Change Conference back in 2009, the increase of 2°C was the threshold for a somewhat sustainable temperature considering the implications of temperature increase. However, that threshold is about to be passed which has led to increasing concerns over the global consequences of the temperature hike.

Committees, commissions, and assemblies have been formed to brainstorm a sustainable solution to this historic and rising threat. And threat it is indeed, since the raising temperature carries many risks that could be catastrophic.

One of the most obvious risks is melting of the ice caps and ice caps resulting in rising sea levels. That leads to an increasing amount of climate migrants as millions of people will be forced to leave their homes that are being invaded by sea, which is rising higher and higher.

There will also be increasing number of extreme heatwaves that will cause havoc and furthermore, far more extreme weather events that have been out there before, such as super hurricanes for example.

The climate change is a new reality that people are learning to cope with. Many of us have probably seen some movies that feature extreme weather events. Things aren't as bad, but they certainly are not very good either.

Another tipping point for permafrost melting reached

There have been earlier warnings by scientist that if the global average temperature would rise just by 2°C, a maximum safe threshold would be reached. In other words, it would be the tipping point after which the climate change would become uncontrollable.

A few decades ago, the tipping points were quite different, such as the Arctic territory becoming free of ice during the summer period. However, the melting permafrost is much more severe problem.

The definition of permafrost is water below freezing point that remains frozen for at least two years nonstop. As trapped carbon was discovered trapped in the Arctic ice, it was deducted that as the ice melted it contributed to greenhouse gas release.

An important keyword here to keep in mind is thawing. It's what happens when ice melts and ground beneath becomes watery or soft. One example of a large-scale transformation based on this phenomenon is Gobi Desert in Mongolia, which has been dry for a long period of time and now becoming much more watery. As a result of thawing, much of the infrastructure built on permafrost becomes affected by it, causing damage to roads and buildings.

The ongoing large-scale permafrost melting is a humongous disaster waiting to happen. As the global temperatures on average are now 3 centigrade higher compared to 20th century's average temperature, the melting is only accelerating.

In order to minimize the damage, infrastructural changes are already underway that aim at absorbing the incoming water, building fortification structures that act as dams in order to slow down the water level increase rate. There are relatively insignificant steps.

Extreme heat waves become the norm in the United States

During the last few decades, the global average temperature has been rising gradually and it's definitely showing across the United States, especially in the regions, such as the States of Utah, Colorado, Arizona and New Mexico.

As the drought intensified, the soil became much less moist. The number of forest fires has also been on the rise.

It's not just the United States where extreme heat waves have been felt. Europe is another spot where previous decades have shown gradual increase in heat wave intensity.

The European Commission's Copernicus Climate Change Service in part reported that the average temperature in Europe as increased by 0.5 centigrade per decade.

People have found various ways to cope with the extreme heatwaves. Some are cranking up their air conditioner, some are cooling in fountains, lakes and rivers and on the beaches. Some are taking more drastic measures and immigrating to colder regions.

The extreme heatwaves are causing lots of damage to crops for instance and they are also causing health issues especially to older generations.

Heatwaves are unfortunately part of the changing climate, which is becoming more in more erratic in many aspects. All we can do at this stage is keep further decreasing our carbon footprint and adapt to the new climate.

All the ocean floor has been mapped

By now, all the ocean floor has been fully mapped. By comparison, mere 20% of the world's ocean floor was mapped. The mapping of the ocean is a large milestone in world exploration achievements as well as a useful resource for better understanding the earth's geology, underwater life and where some hidden oil pockets might be located.

The mapping effort was accomplished through automated ships that were able to traverse the oceans on their own covering hundreds of thousands of square miles. The technical part was done by using sensors and similar pieces of technology. Tethered robots would subsequently be released into the ocean to cover the deepest parts of the oceans.

The acquired data is used for creating detailed online maps, that provide stunningly accurate information on seabeds across the globe, pinpointing the ecological locations of interest, sunken ships, plane wrecks, historical sites, and such. It will also be possible to use the information provided by the maps for reviewing the condition of pipelines, telecommunication cables, remote wind farms and similar offshore structures.

And since the ocean floor has been mapped, the scientific resources that were previously allocated to laborious efforts of handling the sea floor mapping can now be used for something else. Lots of space, for example, is still uncharted.

The idea of "Gene drive mosquitoes" becomes a reality

Throughout the history, the deadliest animal has been an incredibly small insect buzzing around, sucking blood, while sometimes transmitting a disease such as malaria, dengue and yellow fever and many other diseases that resulted over a million of deaths each year.

For thousands of years, these potentially deadly diseases remained in the warm regions across the world, on continents, such as Asia, South and Central America as well as Africa. It wasn't until 2015, when it was reported that due to climate change, these diseases were reaching Europe as well.

Science was harnessed to develop a completely new solution to combat the spreading of these diseases. The solution was to genetically modify the mosquito population in order to eradicate viruses such as malaria.

The genetic modification is implemented through so called gene drives, that are created to modify the inheritance of mosquito population. Through achieving the so-called mutagenic chain reaction, the virus carrying mosquitoes can be eradicated.

This way there is no need to disrupt the natural balance by affecting the food chain simply by exterminating all of mosquitos altogether. The humanity has learned its lesson as to what happens, when you try to eradicate entire species altogether, like what happened in the 50's and 60's of the last century in Latin America. The idea was to get rid of all yellow fever mosquitoes, the same mosquitoes that also spread diseases, such as dengue fever, chikungunya and also zika. After effectively displacing the local mosquito population on a massive scale using different methods, they returned most likely by migrating from different areas. A valuable lesson vas learned.

A volcanic eruption in Japan causes a large disaster

In the early 2000's Japan was one of the most **geologically active places in the world, featuring multiple** annual earthquakes and over 100 active volcanoes.

Sakurajima, an active stratovolcano, which was formed out of an island and has become a peninsula in the Southwestern part of the country is bound to erupt within the six years from 2040.

This estimation is based on the magma supply rate and volume, which accumulates underground.

The last great explosion of Sakurajima happened in 1914, killing 58 people. Nowadays there is technology for early detection of any possible eruptions and thanks to extensive preparations the likelihood is that the casualties will be minimized.

Our planet is constantly moving and changes inside the planet are also constant. Mapping out the tectonic plates, knowing the fault lines and documenting the previous volcanic activities has given us a pretty good idea on the volcanic trends. Needless to say, we cannot predict such events with absolute precision years in advance because it's simply impossible. But with the current tools and technology, we're much better off than what our ancestors were during such events.

There hasn't yet been a technological innovation that would prevent volcanoes from erupting altogether, nor there probably ever will be. At the end of the day, the nature has its final say and there's often very little we can do about it.

The nature runs its course and all we can do is wonder at the events and do our best to try and protect those that are affected by them.

Gulf Coast cities are abandoned due to super hurricanes

The underlying fast increase of carbon dioxide emissions has brought rising sea levels word wide. Adding warming coastal waters to that equation doesn't bode good news for the coastal cities. The climate becomes more volatile.

Super hurricanes have gained presence in the Gulf of Mexico. Every year they wreak havoc causing chaos and destruction to the coastal cities. The windspeed of these super hurricanes can reach up to 200 miles per hour. This leads to uprooted trees and swaying skyscrapers with several buildings losing their roofs, cars being swept away with rapid flash floods along with waves with height of tens of meters.

Each time such disaster occurs the damage cost can rake up to hundreds of billions of dollars. Due to this, several coastal cities are completely abandoned during these super hurricanes. Such cities include Houston and New Orleans.

Needless to say, such unimaginable climatic changes cause waves of so-called climate migrants that move further inland after abandoning their homes.

The hurricanes aren't only expanding in their size but also in territory. As the 21st century progressed from its earlier decades, the hurricanes as well as typhoons gained ground in mid-latitude areas, that encompass cities, such as New York, Boston, Beijing and Tokyo.

These migrating hurricanes could move either north or south of their usual habitat due to climate change. Extreme weather events are also more frequent compared to the previous decades. Governments are scrambling to provide a sufficient response to the new challenge.

Bangkok is largely underwater

Bangkok, which once had a population of many millions now lay underwater. Leading up to 2040 it's been sinking for several decades. As a major metropolis for the millions of its inhabitants, it's a disaster of incredible proportions. At the beginning of 2030's, large areas of Bangkok were already abandoned.

There are quite a few reasons to this tragic outcome. Firstly, the city of Bangkok was originally built on clay. The first settlers that reached the area saw nothing but swamp near the coast.

After several decades of economic growth skyscrapers started to emerge. As the residents of Bangkok consumed water from the groundwater reserves, the soil beneath the buildings became less stable. While the coastline has eroded at the speed of 4 centimetres a year and the monsoon rains have caused to increasingly severe flooding, water became a serious dilemma in Bangkok.

Back in the previous century, land masses were used to block floods and canals were filled to make way to speedy urban construction. Eventually the soft soil of Bangkok could no longer withstand the weight of the increasing amount of city infrastructure built on it.

By the end of 2020's large areas of the city were evacuated, and the former residents found new homes further in the mainland.

Bangkok itself had its days of glory but now what remains are flooded street with high rise buildings slowly succumbing to the elements.

This, in turn, has brought lots of new inhabitants to the territory that has become vacant of human presence, namely animals. Lots of species that are particularly thriving in similar areas are flocking the remains of the city that once was bustling in a whole different way.

Peak phosphorous reached

Phosphorus is one of the most essential building blocks and resources in the world. Phosphorous can be found in DNA as well as in RNA and even in the cell membranes of various living organisms of the flora and fauna around the world.

Unfortunately, phosphorous is not an infinite resource and happens to also be irreplaceable. Alas, the knowledge that this resource is finite there, but it didn't seem like much was done about it.

Peak phosphorous production was reached by the year 2033. This led to staggering inflation, but not only that. Governments started realizing the scale of the issue and started nationalizing the remaining phosphorous and started assigning export tariffs to the product.

The wealthier countries were somewhat more prepared to battle this problem, compared to the less wealthy nations, but still this required a significant change across the world on how to deal with phosphorous. Many new innovations such as urine recycling started contributing as solutions to the issue, although by no means permanent solutions. Others gave considerations to obtaining phosphorous from the seabed.

As the population of the world keeps rising, the substantial challenge is to find a viable alternative to phosphorous. The scientists are already hard at it trying to come up with a new solution that would replace phosphorus, but it's not an easy challenge. The outcome remains to be seen.

Earthquake devastates California

Scientists have said for decades that it's not the question of if the earthquake will hit, it's rather the question of when a large-scale earthquake will strike California, causing damage that can be calculated in billions of dollars, while also causing mass casualties.

The epicentre of this earthquake is in Los Angeles basin, so, Los Angeles suffers considerable amount of the overall damage.

The state of California has seen frequent forest fires, but nothing could prepare it for a sudden shake of the grounds that causes wide scale destruction.

As many might know, when the earthquake magnitude hits a certain threshold on a Richter scale, it starts causing buildings to collapse, trees to be uprooted, causing massive casualties by different type of debris falling down on people for example.

There are a few different ways to prepare for such a disaster. The easiest one is simply to move out of the state. Then there are a number of more complex ways to get prepared, such as rebuilding your house to withstand a strong earthquake.

Earthquakes have been popularized in fictional action movies such as San Andreas. The movies with devastation shown of such massive proportions such as in the movie San Andreas tend to have a result in people saying, "it only happens in movies". However, it's never out of place to think critically of such scepticism. The more we get lulled into the sense of safety, the more we are at risk when it finally hits the fan. And according to major scientific research, it most definitely will.

Social Sphere

Social Credit Score

The social credit score was proven to be a success in the early 21st century. Thus, it has been adopted in most of the countries around the world. It has significantly deterred crime rates and encouraged best social practises in both professional and social encounters.

Bad social credit score limits citizens from conducting some of activities, such as traveling, getting loans, or receiving education, while an exemplary social credit score leads to a wide range of various benefits.

The first country to adopt the social credit score was China, where the full implementation of the social credit score proved to be widely successful.

Many nations have adopted this social credit score, and some are still resisting.

Even though the social credit score is a unique innovation in on itself, we have seen facets of similar arrangement throughout our society. Take for example, the financial sector. All those that have a credit card and are allowed to take credit from their bank automatically get their very own credit score. What that means, is if they at any point default on their ability to pay, their credit score weakens, which in turn will affect their ability to take credit in the future. The ability to pay their credit moves their credit rating up, while the opposite moves it down.

Similar type of approach has been adopted in social media and online games for example, where achievements turn into rewards and breaking the rules can lead to warnings and eventually expulsion.

Universal Basic Income

The massive unemployment in developed countries has been countered with universal basic income. It has eradicated a tremendous amount of poverty in the regions within the UBI´s reach, which comprises of the wealthiest nations on continents such as North America and Europe.

UBI has also improved economy in those regions by boosting the purchase power, thus leading to increased amount of vacant jobs and business driven improvements to the society.

The globally disproportioned welfare has driven floods of migrants to the locations that do provide universal basic income to its citizens.

However, things are not that simple. In order for a person to become privy to the universal basic income, he or she must first accumulate and then maintain a certain social credit score. Then and only then can that person enjoy the privilege of receiving that guaranteed income.

This helps keeping the order in place, by decreasing criminality and encouraging good behaviour.

The amount given each month to each citizen applicable to the UBI, is rather modest, but sufficient for sustaining the livelihood of a singular person. It can also induce boredom or a sense of insignificance. That's why many resort to employment or entrepreneurship.

Increasing Poverty

The regions where there´s no UBI have experienced ever increasing poverty levels with growing slum areas with people living hand to mouth. Such areas are vastly populated, highly polluted and lacking in basic supplies.

Significant increase in poverty has been present especially in the areas affected by devastating effects of climate change. The areas, where fields producing crops have now been submerged by rising water levels have created much poverty, which manifests itself through hunger and migration.

Needless to say, the population growth has played its part in increasing poverty. In addition to that, the increasing scarcity of life sustaining resources and such resources that can be used for trade and harvesting in order to make a living have dwindled in their number.

There have been many initiatives to improve the condition of poorer regions through supporting sustainable farming, looking for new ground water supplies and educating those most at risk of being displaced from the society.

To add to that, the gap between the rich and the poor has grown tremendously. And there doesn't seem to be a cure to that. The less fortunate are just having to cope with the reality on a daily basis. Some of them break free from the chains of poverty and are actually able to make a decent living and some of those may even rise to the riches, but the number of those are very low.

Even though many of the more fortunate countries are trying to offer a helping hand to the less fortunate nations, the issue remains.

Demographics

Demographic shift

Indian, Chinese, and African populations have overlapped the Caucasian population not only in global figures but in context of western hemisphere, also locally, especially in the metropolitan areas.

There are now 8.5 billion people in the world. While the population numbers in developing countries have been steadily increased, the number of citizens of countries like Japan has contrarily decreased. It's been a long while since Japan's 20th century population boom. As of 2010 Japan's population had reached 128 million. That was followed by a gradual and continuous population decline.

By 2042 white people have become the minority in the United States. Other races have overtaken them in the number of births due to a more traditional way of life. The more traditional way of life in this case means traditional family values, in a sense that each individual's duty is to acquire a family and support that family throughout his or her life.

The demographic shift has also brought more cultural variety in the areas that once were constructed of predominantly unipolar western culture. As the fabric of society became more diverse, politicians and legislators had to adapt. For instants hate speech towards certain ethnic groups was outlawed in some western countries.

On the other hand, the cultural adaptation meant that the celebrations, traditions and religion of incoming cultures were in some cases more widely represented.

The shaping of global population

The world population is nearing 9 billion. According to the initial research, year of hitting 9 billion would be 2050 but due to the unprecedented birth rate increase in developing countries like India and also increased life expectancy have resulted in accelerated population growth.

Japan has also been suffering from the lack of work-based immigration. While the country has kept its image as one of the top technological hubs of the world, the locals just haven't prioritized family life to the extent that it would affect population increase. In fact, the average marriage age in Japan has steadily increased and the number of marriages and childbirths have decreased.

At the same time, the western hemisphere has experienced population decline, especially among Caucasian inhabitants. There are now variety of reasons to stay single and enjoy a free and exciting life, which has disrupted the traditional family building scenario.

The urban areas have grown significantly in population while increasing number rural inhabitants have moved to closer to city areas to find more opportunities.

The increasing demand rental housing has driven the prices of rental properties even higher. However, the developers have come up with a new solution for those with tight budget: Micro apartments that are even smaller than studios and subsequently cost less.

Smart houses have become more of a rule than exception. You can now control your home environment with your voice. The surroundings also pick up the signals of your mood and transform accordingly.

Married Couples are now a Minority in the United Kingdom

Following the global trends, the number of marriages has steadily decreased in the UK. This has in turn lead to decreased amount married couples and lessened count of childbirths per woman in the UK.

The reason for this is mainly the lifestyle decision and increased income per capita. Also, considerable reasons are different pressures relating to work, money, as well as the influence of the ambient culture. Staying unmarried no longer labels you the same way it did in the past decades.

The number of married couples has decreased by 9% to 41% total from 2009 among the adult population. This decreasing trend has been followed since 1980's.

Looking at some other causalities we can observe that the transition of social interactions from physical world to virtual has definitely played its part in the decline of marriages. There are also social fringe habits that have become mainstream around messaging, such as ghosting someone, in other words leaving the conversation partner without any notice.

The abundance of sexual pleasures in the virtual world and the more carefree alternatives to having a physical partner have enforced people's decision to remain single or divorced.

Nowadays people can also get a robotic partner that can be tuned for their own particular preference, thus replacing the potentially dysfunctional relationships that so often cause stress amongst the adult population and long-term couples in particular.

Global child mortality has reached 2%

In global population statistics, childhood mortality is the number of children dying before the age of five.

Historically, the child mortality has been a great issue up until the late 20th century. For example, in the 70's, the global average childhood mortality over 14%, while in Africa, it was 24%.

These numbers, however, were decreased during the next years thanks to medicinal developments, improvements in education and work opportunities.

This number seems staggering when comparing to the statistics even hundred years ago. At that time, the solution to high child mortality, as it has been earlier in history, was just to procreate more. In other words, having more children. Families up of over 10 children were not uncommon and in many cases some of those children died before becoming teenagers.

Nowadays, while it is a positive thing that the number of dying toddlers has dropped significantly. One would think that this would have a compounding effect on overpopulation, however, the population growth has slowed down tremendously over the last few decades due to improved quality of life on a global scale, among other things.

Children are highly valuable and the thought of saving them at birth warms everyone's heart. That's why over numerous decades, there has been a breakthrough after breakthrough in biomedical science that have greatly increased our survivability through various adverse situations.

Health

Banning of tobacco

The traditional cigarettes have almost disappeared as the tobacco plants have been eradicated due to health preservation and reserving the land for food production.

Smoke free has become the universal term and tobacco consumption remains only in a few pockets of the world, mainly in developing nations.

According to WHO data, Germany for example had a considerable number of smokers, the total amount of whom in 2021 was approx. 16 million. According to the same research, 127 thousand people lost their lives due to the adverse effects of smoking. Adding to that, Germany happened to have the poorest tobacco control out of 36 countries in Europe and is even far behind countries such as Australia, New Zealand and Brazil.

And it was in 2021, when dozens of health and civil society non-profit organizations launched and strategic incentive for "Tobacco-Free Germany 2040" in form of a publication. The aim was to have a maximum of 5% of adult population of Germany smoking tobacco or electronic cigarettes and less 2% of Germany's adolescent population consuming tobacco products or electronic cigarettes.

Looking at this from the perspective of the year 2040, as it is fictively upon us, Germany has managed to edge much closer to this goal and so have many other nations as well. And so, it is extremely rare to find a person on the street smoking cigarette. In fact, there are only few specially designated areas where smoking is allowed. Thus, such clamping down on smoking has helped further to reduce the numbers of smokers. The world has come a long day since the early days of tobacco to the current more health-conscious society.

Breakthrough in battling diseases

Various diseases that were previously thought to be incurable, have now become easily curable. Alzheimer's disease has long ago become curable. Life expectancies of various cancer patients have been improved tremendously. With the new technology it's possible to add or remove parts of human memory.

The medical research in several medical universities has provided several breakthroughs in treatment of such diseases that were previously deemed uncurable.

When it comes to cancer diseases, bowel cancer happened to be the third most frequent cancer disease according to the statistics. Now, thanks to the recent breakthrough, five-year survival rate for bowel cancer is almost 100%.

These are just examples of how the modern medicine has found solutions to improve human health. Various new treatments, medications and therapies are now available that have passed the clinical trials and been deemed useful and effective.

Many medical cures have also become more affordable to serve larger population. This abundance of various treatment has the human average lifespan especially in developed countries and the human lifespan has expanded due to more sustainable longevity.

The artificial intelligence has an important role in helping develop new solutions to medical problems, although it's not yet self-sustainable as a lot of human resources are working on the issue as well.

Stem cell therapy

Stem cell therapy has reached a whole another level compared to the early 21st century. Stem cell treatment has become so affordable and common that it has gained vast popularity worldwide.

Stem cell treatment in conjunction with gene therapy has not only reversed some of the damages to human body but has led to significant upgrades compared to its normal state.

In fact, by 2031, stem cell pharmacies have become a widespread phenomenon in developed regions of the world. Many of those pharmacies include a comprehensive treatment package that begins with a walk-in diagnosis, which then leads to stem cell collection and banking for future use, in case your younger stem cells will then be necessary for you. You'll experience affordable and tailored treatment for you in order to regenerate some of your body parts and organs.

However, more complex and pricey stem cell treatments are preformed in stem cell clinics and also regular clinics that have an option of treating stem cells.

All-in-all, the stem cell not only helps to reverse some of the damage that your body might have endured, it also rejuvenates it and provides it with longevity and with improved features such as better skin quality.

These days not only the older generations but also the young have found the stem cell therapy useful. There have also been trends around the stem cell treatment, and many have found it even fashionable.

Robotic surgeries

Robotic surgeries have become widespread and manual, human operated surgeries have been banned in all the developed nations and across most of the developing ones.

This has vastly improved the accuracy of the procedures and the turnaround times. The robotic surgeons are also highly profitable for private clinics due to savings in payroll expenses. This has also led to more affordable surgeries, thus adding an increase on already highly incremented human lifespan.

There are of course still human surgeons, especially in countries where the clinics cant afford the robotic surgeon technology, but gradually many more clinics adapt the latest technology.

The robotic surgeons are not simply just the robots themselves, but also the configuration and monitoring software relating to it and of course there's staff involved in maintaining and finetuning the equipment.

The first robotic surgeries were performed in a highly controlled environment, and they were as non-invasive as possible in their nature. A doctor would control robotic arms while monitoring the surgery on a 3D screen. Nurses would also be present to provide any assistance necessary. And also, they mostly consisted of performing tiny incisions or exploring the intestines, for example, to detect possible abnormalities.

Currently surgeons have become almost obsolete as the artificial intelligence is capable of making split second decisions with shocking precision and accuracy.

Updated sports arena

Thanks to genetic trophy, stem cell treatment and bionic implants, some athletes have crossed the transhumanistic boundaries leading to vast debates in various sports oversight groups, whether physical enhancement is considered a fair attribute to a human body. This is because such transhumanism or human synthesis has made the athletes faster, stronger, smarter and more endurable which gives them a significant advantage compared to biologically unenhanced human competitors.

As it stands, in 2036 the Olympics committee has launched a new "super athlete" category, where athletes enhanced with bionic implants are free to participate. These transhuman athletes made a showcase participation category back in 2036 but are now becoming more and more established part of the Olympic world.

Technical and pharmaceutical companies have chosen to sponsor these athletes due to the profound marketing opportunity arising from such action.

When it comes to the spectators, they have the option to follow the sporting events, in virtual reality even in real time if they choose to do so.

The range of sports has also increased. The viewers have more entertainment options than ever before in the sports world.

New world records emerge as the previous world records get smashed by superior athletes.

Bionic Implants

The bionic implants have become fashionable and convenient addition to human physiology. While limb implants for those who lost one in an accident for example, allow full motoric of a standard functionality of a real limb, there are also other bionic body parts that extend the abilities of those that come as a standard and a natural counterpart.

For example, bionic eyes have brought relief for visually impaired individuals and those willing to extend the capabilities of their eyesight. One can purchase an eye with an eyesight so accurate, it could compete with that of an eagle.

Bionic implants also have different functionalities, like a touch screen on your arm, ability to play your favourite music, without carrying an iPod, call an Uber and many other things.

Bionic engineering has also provided technology for regenerating bionic implants and non-implanted body parts, such as limbs for example.

It wasn't easy at all for the general public to adapt to the idea that you could integrate body parts that were fully functional or enhanced. It would be typical of something you would generally see in a science fiction movie. But nevertheless, bit by bit people adapted and many decided to take their own bionic enhancement just to brag to their friends.

There of course is an age limitation as to who can take bionic implants, which is banned from children unless they medically need it and receive a full approval from their parents.

Synthetic human genome is achieved

Way back in 2010, the first artificial lifeform was made by scientists. It was called Mycoplasma laboratorium. It was a new type of bacteria with human created genetic code that was designed on a computer and fitted in a synthetic chromosome and then placed in an empty cell. This way the cell acquired its very own software, through which it could create proteins and create new cells.

Six year later, a minimal bacterial genome was created, which was a milestone in this development trajectory. A couple months later a "Human Genome Project – Write "was announced that aimed to understand the DNA code. The subsequent HGP – Write project on the other hand was meant to create new code, while producing new DNA chains.

The possibility to synthesise large parts of human genome paves way to many innovations in medical, agricultural energy and other sectors. Technically, this technology even allows cloning of humans. There have definitely been lots of cloning experiments in the past, but there has never been a successful cloning of a human. Needless to say, such endeavour would be strictly banned. However, some underground laboratories secretly conduct their illegal experiments relating to this as well.

From the medical perspective, this revolutionizes the treatment of those whose limbs have been amputated for example. There are countless different medical applications based upon this scientific breakthrough and in many ways, this is only the tip of the iceberg.

Food and Water

Plant based meat is dominating the meat market

As we are in 2040, half a century ago, there was a lot of speculation about sufficiency of the food resources in the future, meat in particular. However, an alternative has been found from vegan meat replacement. The plant-based product had its troubles of acquiring acceptance among the general public, but gradually it gained traction and even became a mainstream product.

When it comes to plant-based food production and distribution, there are a few leading corporations that are the main players in the marketplace, with their revenues measured in billions of dollars, while the smaller competitors are fighting for single digit market shares globally at best.

The necessity for plant-based meat began when it became obvious that cows produce lots of methane and thus contribute to the global warming.

For thousands of years, the meat market products have been primarily originated from cows, pigs, chickens and such. There has been a significant industry around that. And obviously when the government has made moves on restricting the meat production, there has been significant amount of pushback from the farmers in particular that produce that meat.

One particular part of the audience that is very thrilled about this innovation are the vegans that can finally sink their teeth into some meat products, now that they are plant based.

Widespread high scale production has already been established for plant-based meat, which is also more sustainable environmentally and which also has longer shelf life.

Drinking water scarcity

Drinking water has become an increasingly scarce commodity. As the population growth and global warming have placed increasing a burden on fresh water sources, especially in the equatorial and surrounding regions on continents like Asia and Africa, people are struggling to acquire this precious liquid that is the necessary proponent to their survival.

Needless to say, the water retail companies have spotted the high demand but are most commonly inclined to increase their profitability by incrementing the water prices rather than acting as humanitarian proponents through making the water more available through its increased affordability.

Now being 2040, the water withdrawal rate has reached 4,000 billion cubic meters. On the other hand, the water consumption has reached over 1,700 billion cubic meters.

For decades, global water stress status has been measured by calculating the ratio of withdrawals to supply. Those countries with highest ratios are also the most stressed. Currently, those are the countries of the Middle East, northern Africa, parts of the southern Africa, Patagonia, and Central Asia. In those regions, the ratio of withdrawals to supply has been measured to be over 80%, which is extremely high by comparison.

In the face of this growing issue, many inventors have tried to come up with a highly scalable invention that transforms seawater into drinking water. Some breakthroughs on a minor scale have been made, but nothing that could be scaled for consumption of millions of people has yet been produced.

Transportation

Self-driving cars

Self-driving electric cars are now widely spread around the world. Means of public transportation has reshaped itself technologically in way that optimizes ambience and comfort. While the exterior design of the car is optimally aerodynamic, the interior parts reflect comfort with a minimalistic style and smart features.

The car is plugged into the A.I. network and you can have discussions with it whenever you feel like it. If you feel like sleeping, or prefer privacy while you commute, you can tell your car to dim your windows.

Driving the car is not permitted with a few exceptions and depending on location. More developed nations are obviously more regulated, while some of the developing countries still allow drivers to have full control of their vehicles.

The automobile industry is no longer producing vehicles with combustion engine running on fuel such as gasoline. The cars are powered by electricity and their charging efficiency has been steadily improving ever since the prototypes of Fisker Karma or Tesla were launched.

There now are no drivers in the self-driving cars, just passengers. There are various ways they can entertain themselves during the trip. That includes movies, games, and music.

Since the self-driving cars are operated by software, there have been valid concerns about hacking cars and causing casualties through manipulating it. Keeping that in mind, companies and software developers have come up with guardrails that make it more and more difficult to cause a malicious outcome.

Airplane innovations

The interiors of airplanes nowadays remind of a high-end hotel lobby. The flight times are also much shorter compared to what they once used to be.

And believe it or not, many airplanes now run-on electricity.

And I'll take it one step further: Several plane types are windowless! However, you do see what's outside.

What you see, is a plane that is made from uber-light smart screen panels. This means you have almost 360 degrees view of the world outside of the airplane.

In Norway by 2040 all civil aviation has become electric. Single charge voyages have become possible thanks to solid-state batteries with 650Wh/kg of energy density. The lithium-ion cells are equipped in plane's fuselage and wings.

So all-in-all, the airplane voyage has been transformed to a more diverse experience that is also more environmentally friendly compared to what it was decades before.

Planes have also much more variety of entertainment available for the passengers. For example, instead of watching the movies or listening to the music or playing two dimensional games, they can immerse in virtual reality and handle their daily business with high-speed internet connection or entertain themselves with fully immersive video games or other types of entertainment.

Planes have also been made much more secure and faster compared to the previous types. These innovations aren't equal everywhere in the world, so many travel just to experience them.

Flying Cars are Widespread in Urban Surroundings

By the end of 2030's the so-called urban air mobility industry has reached trillion-dollar market value. The market share is divided between various car and airline companies.

The progression of urban air mobility began in the previous decades with both military and civilian drone equipment. Then came the vertical take-off and landing vehicles, or so-called VTOL's along with the postal drones.

With the recent safety improvements in 2040, the VTOL is a secure and fast way to commute from place to place as compared to road transportation.

These vehicles are fully autonomous and can be private or as a peer-to-peer business derived transport option working much like Uber at its early stages.

The development of these small flying methods of transportation has affected the urban planning requiring the construction of specific parking areas for them in the premises near residential and commercial spaces.

These "flying cars", if you will, run on electricity. In other words, they are fully environmentally friendly, made largely out of lightweight composite material and are incredibly durable.

Many of us have read books, watched movies, cartoons or read comic books about how cars would be flying in the future, but experiencing it in person is something different altogether.

Hyperloop

The future of transportation that a Billionaire entrepreneur Elon Musk had envisioned came into major fruition about 10 years ago. In 2030, Musk´s hyperloop tube capsule was able to reach a staggering 600 miles per hour speed. Also, the fees became more affordable for the average consumer. This created a viable alternative to air travel.

So, this is how it works. You go underground, you go inside a capsule sized less than a train cart. You sit comfortably, strap in, announcement is made and soon you'll be on your way going faster than a bullet train.

In addition to Elon Musk´s North American Hyperloop, there are many competing Hyperloop firms across the globe, providing transportation at an affordable rate.

Hyperloop makes sense economically, because it's cheaper than a plane, but travels somewhat as fast. The Hyperloop technology is also safe and efficient. You prevent being stuck in traffic during the rush hour.

The technology is relatively simple. Magnetic pods are levitating inside a tube and being thrust at incredible speed with its propulsion system, incurring no friction due to removal of ambient air inside the adjacent tubes encapsulating the pods. This is the key advantage of Hyperloop over the older models of maglev trains.

The Hyperloop technology is constantly developing to become the travel faster, safer and interactive, in other words a more pleasant experience for the passengers.

Northeast Corridor high-speed rail route completed

In year 2040 the high-speed speed railway is still under construction. This railway spans between Boston and Washington D.C. The main purpose of the high-speed railroad is to decrease the duration between Boston and Washington D.C. In fact, this high-speed improvement will shorten the travel from 6:17 hours to 3:05 hours.

The high-speed trains would move at up to 220 mph. This is poised to increase the number of passengers, many of which would use it as a daily commute to and from work.

This type of infrastructural remedy to national transportation issues such as traffic jams is long overdue. Local officials have been trying to improve public transportation to increase the number of commuters and thus benefiting from the income produced by that.

Depending on how successful the rollout of the Northeast Corridor is, similar corridors may follow suit, but that is yet to be seen.

The north-eastern part of the United States has a particular significance because that's where the metropolitan hubs are located with high density population. Also, lots of the population in cities like New York use the public transport to commute to work, so building a high-speed railway in that area was a natural solution.

These new trains provide more luxury than the previous models. There's more leg space and the chairs are more comfortable. You can also select from a range of different beverages and snacks while you're moving at a comparatively high speed on the train.

Helsinki-Tallinn tunnel has been completed

An undersea tunnel stretching almost 30 miles under the Gulf of Finland. It has become the longest undersea tunnel in the world, exceeding the Channel tunnel connecting England and France under the English Channel.

The tunnel stretches between the Finnish Helsinki-Vantaa airport with Ulemiste aiport of Estonia. Tunnel stations can also be found in Pasila and Helsinki city center.

The tunnel can be accessed for example through an inclined access point, in other words a spiral shaped tunnel that on Finnish side can be accessed from an artificial island. There are two artificial islands between the tunnel route: Uppoluoto and Tallinnamodal.

The tunnel framework will consist of 3 running tubes with diameters of 8 meters and 10 meters for maintenance tunnel and two running tubes respectively. At its deepest point, the tunnel runs 250 meters under the sea surface. There will be 3 types of trains: passenger trains, car and truck shuttle trains and freight trains.

The purpose of the tunnel was to grow the leisure and business opportunities between the two countries. The 2-hour ferry transportation time has now been cut to just 30-minute train travel which has exponentially grown the day tourism and work commuting, particularly in the number of passengers traveling back and form between Tallinn and Helsinki.

Cargo Sous Terrain construction is nearing its completion

The term "Cargo Sous Terrain" might be unknown to most people. It means an automated freight transport system that exists underground. It's located in Switzerland and its objective is to minimize the excessive traffic on the roads, which has increased tremendously over the last few decades.

This network of underground tubes consists of self-driving transport carts and transfer stations. The cost of this project was 35 billion dollars, and it was funded by private capital.

The first tube network section is located between Härkingen-Niederbipp and Zurich and it spans through a length of 43 miles including 10 hubs distributed between the two areas.

By 2045 there will be 80 hubs and the network will span throughout the width of the entire country.

The tunnels will feature above-ground waystations accompanied by vertical lifts, that allow for quick cargo transfer. Each transport enables refrigeration of cargo. This is essential, particularly for daily consumables and medicine.

The underground vehicles run on renewable energy. They get their power from electromagnetic induction and can reach the speed of 10 miles per hour. They operate non-stop and provide automatic loading and also unloading of goods. There is also an auxiliary system for packages that operates on monorail and is located at the tunnel ceiling level with twice the velocity compared to the vehicles below.

In essence, Cargo Sous Terrain provides a more efficient, silent and pollution free transport of goods while decreasing the road traffic.

Driverless flying taxis can be spotted everywhere

It started in the second decade of 21st century. Then, you could spot something quite extraordinary: a mix between a helicopter and a drone when you looked up in Dubai.

These Autonomous Air Taxis were capable of reaching the speed of 100 kilometers per hour and didn't need you to be a pilot for you to be the only human in them while they are moving through the air.

The vehicle consisted of a cabin with 18 rotos giving it enough lift to transport even a heavy load with intelligent autonomous control system that does not need external assistance to move passengers between different locations.

The innovation that became operational around 20 years ago is now commonplace among multiple self-driving vehicles in the city.

The idea of having a driverless taxi probably came from some futuristic sci-fi movies whereas it is common for the science fiction genre, the future looks very futuristic.

However, for 2040 this type of tech is nothing new, because driverless vehicles and flying cars have been around for a while. Getting a taxi could not be easier and it appears at your doorstep within minutes.

These taxis are also quite affordable, especially the used vehicles that are based on peer-to-peer business model like Uber. There are also luxury rides such as flying limos that are of course far more expensive compared to those mentioned earlier. But they are reserved for the few and wealthy.

ICE transition into battery-electric shipping

During the 2030's battery-electric propulsion becomes commercially feasible and many commercial shipping routes start taking advantage of this new technological advancement. As a tradeoff, they're moving away from the yesterday's technology, the internal combustion engine or the so-called ICE.

As the transition kicks in newer as well as older ships dump their engines and electrify their engines. Some are taking the hybrid option, but more and more vessels go fully electric, because the early perceptions of clumsy, costly, and not so practical battery-electric drive are shattered through successful examples of electrified sea vehicles.

This transformation process was sparked by green efforts of moving off the internal combustion engines and thus to safeguard our planet. As the first countries adopted this approach, more and more nations made it feasible for the ships to undergo this transformation.

For the passengers, this transformation is largely invisible. However, it can be heard. You no longer hear the sound of loud engines. It all runs smoothly and quietly. The ships are also more efficient and there are less maintenance troubles due to engine problems. The battery-electric drives are also much more lightweight and durable.

Some sceptic minds might doubt, how the battery-electric vessels can travel for weeks at a time without running out of juice. Well, thanks to widespread use of solar panels and the ability to recharge the batteries the vessel can basically sail infinitely.

Even lots of private vessels have been equipped with this new technology and it has definitely become a big hit in the market.

Culture

All J.R.R. Tolkien's works are about to enter public domain

The legendary author J.R.R. Tolkien who invented the mythological world of the Middle Earth also had his works protected under copyright. This copyright is set to expire in 2044 thus fully entering the public domain.

When author's works enter public domain, it basically means that anyone whatsoever is completely at freedom to use them in whichever way they please. This includes creating different versions of it in a film or theatre production, reprinting the books, creating new varieties of the fanfiction, coming up with video games and so on. The main takeaway of this, that whoever is free to profit from any of the production that is derived publications that enter the public domain.

This is great news to many enthusiastic and creative fans that can't wait to start working on their own version of the fantasy publications.

As some of the most passionate Tolkien fans know, there are quite a few more books published that were authored by Tolkien that the public doesn't know about. They might not be as legendary as the most famous pieces of his literature, but nevertheless as creative and as unique.

The fantasy genre is always a very inspiring place to go to, to read unforgettable books and to craft inspiring literature. It's something that has always been attributed to humans and yet the artificial intelligence isn't capable of doing that. Someday it might, but until then, the fantasy land is a busy place to be.

Possible Prediction Issues

Inaccurate predictions

Sometimes predictions simply go wrong. A good example is a prediction that was on one of my most prominent sources: *Futuretimeline.net*.

The prediction was, that Xbox 360 would be followed by an Xbox 720. It turned out, that that the successor of the console was named Xbox One. In my view, this is a case where linear probability does not pan out as expected in logical fashion. Instead,

...there´s always the unexpected...

to quote a famous line in Bridge of the River Kwai.

Reasons why there MIGHT NOT BE A YEAR 2040 for us

Yes. I wrote the last words in caps lock. One cannot understate the possibility of the end of the world as we know it. A human extinction, due to perhaps one of the following reasons is a very distant possibility, but a possibility, nevertheless.

The reasons being:

- A catastrophic event
    - A massive comet hitting the earth
    - A highly contagious and lethal super virus
- A nuclear war

References:

https://www.cnbc.com/2018/04/25/ai-could-lead-to-a-nuclear-war-by-2040-rand-corporation-warns.html

https://www.forbes.com/pictures/lmj45ighg/no-2-postal-service-mail-sorters-carriers-and-clerks/#6c5422eb495d

https://www.alux.com/jobs-gone-automation-ai/

https://www.thesun.co.uk/tech/4115579/self-driving-cars-robot-lovers-future-in-2040/

https://pixabay.com/fi/ravintola-flirttailu-pari-kippis-1807617/

https://www.futuretimeline.net/21stcentury/2040.htm

https://www.quantumrun.com/future-timeline/2040

https://www.futuretimeline.net/21stcentury/2040.htm#china-nuclear-shuttles

https://pixabay.com/photos/cash-currency-financial-investment-3829601/

https://pixabay.com/illustrations/vortex-fusion-violet-blue-1264042/

https://www.futuretimeline.net/21stcentury/2036.htm#transhuman-athletes-2036-2040

https://thehill.com/opinion/technology/386524-the-west-could-be-closer-to-chinas-system-of-social-credit-scoring-than

https://www.futuretimeline.net/21stcentury/2034.htm#robots

https://www.futuretimeline.net/21stcentury/2035.htm#alien-life

https://edition.cnn.com/travel/article/how-long-hyperloop/index.html

https://www.arch2o.com/denmark-germany-under-hour-hyperloop-technology/

https://www.ttnews.com/articles/should-self-driving-cars-be-road-safety-regs-are-place-dianne-feinstein-says-no

https://www.bbc.com/future/article/20180814-norways-plan-for-a-fleet-of-electric-planes

https://www.theguardian.com/business/2014/oct/26/innovations-windowless-plane#img-1

https://www.themanufacturer.com/articles/top-jobs-in-2040-will-involve-virtual-reality-artificial-intelligence-robotics/

https://www.iflscience.com/technology/elon-musk-claims-neuralink-could-render-human-language-obsolete-in-five-to-ten-years/

https://futuristspeaker.com/future-of-work/20-common-jobs-in-2040/

https://arvrjourney.com/holographic-tv-is-coming-on-its-way-will-the-future-be-bright-ad23863c4bbc

New Interactive, Holographic AI Can Adapt To Your Personality (futurism.com)

https://www.statista.com/statistics/216527/global-demand-for-water/#:~:text=It%20is%20projected%20that%20global%20water%20demand%20will,likely%20to%20vary%20based%20on%20region%20and%20sector

https://tunnelcontact.com/groups/profile/10484/finest-finland-estonia-helsinki-tallinn-tunnel-project#:~:text=FinEst%20Link%20or%20Talsinki%20tunnel%20is%20the%20proposed,for%20deepening%20economic%20co-operation%20between%20Helsinki%20and%20Tallinn.

https://www.wri.org/insights/ranking-worlds-most-water-stressed-countries-2040

https://blogs.bmj.com/tc/2021/09/13/a-strategy-for-tobacco-free-germany-2040/

https://news.yale.edu/2022/01/03/future-hurricanes-will-roam-over-more-earth-study-predicts

https://edition.cnn.com/2016/02/05/health/zika-virus-kill-all-mosquitoes/index.html

https://en.wikipedia.org/wiki/Laws_of_robotics

https://en.wikipedia.org/wiki/Carbon_nanotube#Applications

https://en.wikipedia.org/wiki/16K_resolution

https://www.nasa.gov/content/exploring-the-depths-of-titan-s-seas

https://www.freethink.com/space/deorbit-iss

https://en.wikipedia.org/wiki/Digital_currency

https://www.forbes.com/advisor/in/investing/digital-currency-in-india/

https://www.sciencedirect.com/topics/engineering/hydrogen-energy

https://indiaenergyportal.org/hydrogen-energy/

https://www.analyticssteps.com/blogs/how-artificial-intelligence-ai-can-be-used-politics-government

www.ingramcontent.com/pod-product-compliance
Lightning Source LLC
Chambersburg PA
CBHW071551120726
48009CB00001B/3